Embracing Autism

The Keys to Understanding,
Accepting, and Embracing Autism

Copyright © 2018 by Kaylene George

All rights reserved. This book or any portion thereof may not be reproduced or used in any manner whatsoever without the express written permission of the publisher except for the use of brief quotations in a book review.

Printed in the United States of America
First Printing, 2018

ISBN 978-1-7322912-0-1

Kaylene George
PO Box 99219
Spokane, Washington 19566

www.AutisticMama.com

DISCLAIMER:
The author of this book is an autistic parent of an autistic child, not a therapist, doctor, or other autism professional. None of the recommendations, thoughts, or opinions in this book are intended to replace professional opinion. Please discuss what you learn in this book with your family's autism professionals.

This book is dedicated first and foremost to my son, A-Man. We've been in this journey to *Embracing Autism* together and I am unbelievably proud of the sweet boy that he's becoming every single day. His autism has taught me so much about him, about myself, and about the world.

I'd also like to dedicate this book to my wonderful husband, Chris, who handles all of my autistic quirks with grace and love, and to all of my kids, Mr. C, A-Man, Cap'n M, Miss S, and Sweet C for surviving this year with mommy's nose buried in her laptop!

Table of Contents

Dedication

Chapter 1 - My Journey to Embracing Autism

Chapter 2 - You Need an Autism Tribe

Chapter 3 - It's Okay to Feel However You Feel

Chapter 4 - Focusing on the Positives for Your Child

Chapter 5 - The Many Benefits of Autism

Chapter 6 - Understanding Autism Meltdowns and How to Handle Them

Chapter 7 - Fighting and Advocating for Autistics

Chapter 8 - Everything You Really Need to Know About Functioning Labels

Chapter 9 - Evaluating Autism Organizations

Chapter 10 - Why and How to Listen to Autistic Self-Advocates

Chapter 11 - Understanding the Importance of Identity Language

Chapter 12 - Remember, Autistics Have Joy

Chapter 13 - Final Thoughts on Embracing Autism

Terms to Know and Further Reading

Acknowledgements

Chapter 1
My Journey to Embracing Autism

When my son A-Man was about 18 months old he changed. He stopped talking. He stopped singing. He stopped looking in people's eyes. He stopped eating 95% of foods, foods he previously loved. He had extreme meltdowns like you wouldn't believe. Or, you probably would believe me, since you're reading this book and I'm guessing that means that your child has meltdowns too.

I approached his pediatrician about this regression, and she gave me every excuse in the book. It was because I divorced my husband and moved into a new home. It was because I didn't "make him" eat. It was because his older brother talked for him and I didn't "make him" talk. It was because he was a younger sibling and his big brother was advanced. Every. Possible. Excuse.

Eventually I pleaded with her. If she would give us a referral to a speech therapist, I promised I would give up. If the speech therapist agreed that his regression was only because of my parenting, I would stop badgering. She begrudgingly agreed and was sure that the speech therapist would laugh off my concerns.

The speech therapist didn't laugh.

In fact, the speech therapist said that there was "very clearly something going on" and recommended that we begin working with an occupational therapist and get on the waiting list for a neurodevelopmental pediatrician to seek further diagnosis. The therapists cannot diagnose, of course, but she did want me to be prepared that A-Man had definite signs of a disorder called dyspraxia that causes motor functioning delays, and that he also could possibly fall on the autism spectrum.

We spent about six months seeing the speech and occupational therapists while waiting to see the neurodevelopmental pediatrician. In that time I remarried and begun to further expand our family. Finally it was time for our appointment. Our therapists warned me that sometimes it can take several appointments and tests before they give an official diagnosis. We met with the doctor for about an hour. She observed A-Man, read our therapists' reports, and interviewed me about his typical behavior, his birth, and anything else she found relevant. We left her office with an official diagnosis.

After six months of therapy and research, no one was particularly shocked to learn that A-Man was officially autistic. While the doctor was prepared for me to be upset and shocked, I just thanked her and discussed our next steps.

Little-by-little as I started researching and learning more, I realized that I wasn't the typical autism mom, and I didn't want to be. I learned about the horrors of certain autism organizations. As I joined groups for parents of autistic kids, I started realizing that a lot of parents truly hated their child's autism and wanted to find "cures" for it. I learned about the debate of identity language vs. person-first language and the wide divide between parents of autistic children and autistic people themselves.

I found myself siding with autistic self-advocates over parents of autistic kids on many of these issues. I had been told over and over again that it was only because my son was considered "high functioning" (don't worry, we'll chat more about that later). They said that if my child was more severe I'd understand why they so desperately wanted to cure their child's autism or why they saw it as such a tragedy. I wasn't convinced, but I really couldn't put my finger on why it was so easy for me to agree with autistic adults.

Then one day it all changed. It started as a random conversation with one of my good friends. I was talking about my extreme dislike for change and a few other things that caused me extreme anxiety, and how that helped me to understand and be more empathetic with A-Man than most people. My friend interrupted me, *"Don't take this the wrong way, but, are you on the spectrum as well?"* she asked. I wasn't sure how to respond. Could I be on the spectrum? I had never thought about it before. I mean, I was an adult. Surely if I was autistic I would know, right? Someone would have known? Plus, while I could recognize some major similarities between myself and A-Man, there were also major differences. I could make eye contact with people. It was extremely uncomfortable and often downright painful, but I could do it. I had a lot of friends growing up. I mean, I often felt like I wasn't quite "getting it", but I had a lot of friends.

I told Chris, my new husband, about the conversation half-kidding to get a feel for what he thought. We both knew that I had really extreme anxiety, but autism? We'd never really considered it. I started doing some more research. This time, specifically about adult diagnosis and the difference in how female autistics present than male autistics. I talked with a sweet friend of mine who was diagnosed as an adult after getting her son's diagnosis. I went through diagnostic criteria with several people who knew me to be sure it wasn't just me reading too much into things.

It turns out I'm autistic. I found out at 23 years old, as a mother of four children. Suddenly, it made sense how I ended up on the wrong side of the river that separates autistic self-advocates and parents of autistic children. I was in this odd position of both. I am autistic and my son is autistic. Immediately, I knew that I wanted to share all that I know with people on both sides of that river. My goal was to eventually build a bridge, so that parents and autistic selfadvocates can be on the same page and work together. This book? It's the first step in building that bridge.

In this book you'll find the secrets I've learned in the past few years since my son and I were diagnosed. We'll walk hand-in-hand through beginning to understand your child's diagnosis, to accepting it, and eventually embracing it. This process will take time. There will be times in this book that you put it down and think that I'm crazy. You might read a chapter and think *"well that's because she doesn't understand an autistic child like mine."* Just a side note, I assure you, the main point throughout this book is that each child with autism is different and that's okay!

I encourage you to work through the book even when your gut instinct doesn't agree with me. I challenge you to keep reading, even when something I say makes you uncomfortable. When this book challenges your deeply held beliefs about autism, and disabilities in general, think about why what I'm saying is upsetting you. Take some time to try and see the point and the heart behind the words. Know that I truly want to help you go from the traditional autism parent to a true autism advocate. I want you to become an effective and strong advocate and ally for your child. This way, when your autistic child becomes an autistic adult, they will see that you did absolutely everything you possibly could to meet their needs.

Please know that I'm thinking of you often, and I would love to help you through this incredible journey towards embracing autism. You can do this. You were made to be your child's parent, and I know that just by purchasing this book you've made an incredible step towards love, understanding, acceptance, and truly embracing your child for exactly who they are.

Chapter 2
You Need an Autism Tribe

Now that I've introduced myself and shared some of my journey with autism, I wanted to address the fact that you can't do this alone because although autism is wonderful, it's also challenging. I know that someone telling you 'autism is wonderful' when you're in the middle of meltdowns and battles with insurance companies and struggles with your child's IEP meetings might seem ridiculous. What I hope you'll learn through this book is that it is true. There's many wonderful things about autism, and in time they will outweigh the struggles and the fear that you may be facing.

That said, there will always be challenges. Whether your child is considered high functioning or low functioning by professionals, you and your child will face your own unique struggles. Maybe your child has aggressive meltdowns during everyday transitions (my son sure did) or maybe you're struggling with a child who bolts when you're in a parking lot. Whatever the challenges you're facing, with time, you will find ways for you, and your children, to cope.

What's important to keep in mind is that as your child ages and your understanding of autism grows, your challenges will change, but they will not go away. When we first got A-Man's diagnosis, our biggest struggle was with extreme meltdowns during transitions. Now? His meltdowns have changed and he doesn't scream or get as aggressive as he used to, but he yells mean things at us when he loses control.

You Need a Tribe that Understands

I cannot emphasize enough how important it is to have a tribe that truly understands autism and your particular child. On particularly rough days, you'll want to fall back on that tribe to vent. It's important that your tribe understands and loves your autistic child because you need to be able to say to them *"if I have to manage another meltdown today I'm going to lose it,"* and know that they will offer support and love, not judgment or ignorant comments.

The simplest way to find a tribe that will really understand is to build your tribe with other parents of autistic kids. They understand the ins and outs of meltdowns, elopement, IEPs, therapies, and more. They'll have real advice that actually has a chance of working with your kids, rather than parents of neurotypical kids saying things like "I'd never let my kid do that". In the end, it's just a huge gift to have a solid tribe of a few parents of autistic kids in your corner. Whether you find these parents in an online group, through your child's therapy clinic, or you're just lucky enough to know several parents of autistic kids, get yourself a tribe!

Beyond that tribe, you should also work on making your traditional tribe more understanding about your child and autism. When I say traditional tribe, I think about your spouse, your immediate family, your friends, your child's teachers and friends, and the people you are in contact with every day. While these may not end up being the people that you bring your autism vents to, they can be invaluable when it comes to general support. When you need a babysitter for your other kids while you take your autistic child to therapy, or you need a break from all things autism and want to go have a girls night, you will need your friends and family around.

How to Help Your Tribe Understand Autism

The million dollar question is how to promote an understanding of autism in your tribe members. Your tribe can't be very helpful if they have no idea what you and your child are going through. It can be really difficult for people without personal experience with autism to reach a true understanding. While most people these days are aware of autism, at least at a stereotypical level, that doesn't necessarily mean that they understand or are comfortable with autistic people. For example, someone might support "autism awareness" campaigns, but that same person might become extremely uncomfortable when your child flaps his or her arms happily while you're out together in public.

Tons and tons of open conversations are going to be your best bet to help your tribe understand autism. We got A-Man's diagnosis a few years ago, and Chris and I regularly still have discussions about how his autism affects our parenting. With every change we face in A-Man's development, we have to change our approach with him slightly, and I feel like the conversations will never end. Similarly, I regularly talk with our extended family about autism and what it means for our family. I spend a lot of time at family functions explaining why A-Man does what he does, where the behaviors are coming from, and what types of expectations are reasonable or unreasonable for them to have.

I'm not telling you it's going to be easy. We still have serious struggles with helping people understand A-Man and his autism. We get asked at family functions if he ever eats "real food" and we're questioned fairly regularly about why we're so strict with Mr. C when it seems like A-Man has no rules. That said, we've made some real breakthroughs in the last few years. At a party recently my sister saw A-Man stimming at the table and said, *"He does that when he's happy, so I know he's doing okay."* It was a simple observation to her, but to us it meant the world.

Working with Doctors, Therapists, and School Staff

While not traditionally a part of your "tribe", working with doctors, therapists, school staff, and aides is going to be a huge part of your future. You'll be working with these people to create care plans and IEPs, accommodations and recommendations. Trust me when I say that a good therapist will become your best friend, and a terrible doctor can quickly become your worst enemy. Thankfully, along the way we've found a few tips that help us work with this part of our autism tribe.

My first and biggest tip is to know that if you are clashing with one of these people, you can always seek out other options. If your therapist is doing something that you don't like, you can find another therapist. If your child's doctor is fighting you about referrals that you know your child needs, you can switch doctors. If your child's teacher is not following their IEP, you can request a classroom switch. A-Man's pediatrician fought us for way too long before allowing us to see a speech therapist, and we wasted so much time that could have been spent learning about and beginning to understand his autism.

I will admit, though, it isn't always easy to just replace the professionals in your child's life. In many towns the therapy options are limited, and your insurance may leave your choice in doctor pretty restricted. When you're doing your best to make it work with the hand you're dealt, there are a few things you can do to make your experience (and your child's) a lot better.

The first thing you should do is make your beliefs and expectations clear. When we encounter a new professional, we have a lengthy discussion about my views on autism. We make it clear to them that we don't see autism as a tragedy and that we require respect for our child and his autistic traits. Any therapies that seek to make him act more neurotypical aren't welcome in our family. It's important for every therapist that we work with to know that. Make sure you're ready to really stand up for your beliefs. We don't follow the standard care plan that most autism families do. We homeschool, we don't do ABA therapy, and we embrace autistic tendencies, so we have to be ready to face some push back from professionals that are used to the status quo. Always keep in mind that your child is your child, and you are doing what's best!

Advocate Highlight: **Amy Sequenzia**

Amy Sequenzia is a non-speaking autistic activist and writer. Amy writes on her blog about disability rights and respect for disabled people. She's on the board of directors of the Autistic Self Advocacy Network (ASAN), the Florida Alliance for Assistive Services and Technology (FAAST), and Autism Women's Network.
You can learn more about Amy at *Ollibean.com*

Chapter 3
It's Okay to Feel However You Feel

This chapter is a difficult one to write. It's a really difficult balance that I feel is missing a lot with most autism resources available now. See, in the books and blog posts written by parents, this chapter tends to be their main focus. They tell you to grieve the child you thought you'd have and to take as long as you need to feel sad. On the flip side, resources written by autistic self-advocates tend to gloss over this section. We talk about how autism isn't a negative thing, and you should just accept it.

I'm in a unique position in that I'm a parent and an autistic self-advocate. I understand the need for a delicate balance in a resource like this. It is okay for you to feel sad, but you also need to know that autism isn't a negative thing, and you'll soon see the beauty. I do my best in this book to address both of these sides, while realizing that it may take you some time, and a lot of processing, to learn to understand, accept, and embrace your child's autism.

So I'll write this chapter the best I can. I hope that you find some comfort in the words.

Autism is Shocking

When we got an autism diagnosis for our son, it wasn't incredibly shocking. But that's only because it took us over 6 months after we learned he was autistic to get an appointment with the right doctor to officially diagnose him. While we were waiting to see the doctor, when his therapist first mentioned autism, I was in complete shock. I knew something had caused the sudden regression, but surely my son wasn't autistic.

Thankfully, after more research and more talks with his very patient therapists, we started to understand that autism truly is a spectrum. Some autistic people communicate by speaking, others do not. Some autistic people can make eye contact, others cannot, and still others can but choose not to. There is no cut and dry set of traits that will fit every autistic person. As I slowly grew in my understanding of autism, suddenly a whole new world was opened up. Not only did I start to realize and accept that my son was autistic, but it lead to the realization about my own autism about a year later.

Regardless of whether you learned when your child was six months, six years, or sixteen years old, it can initially be a shock. That's perfectly okay. Let yourself feel shocked and surprised. Ignore people who said *"of course they're autistic, they've always done x."* Also, ignore people who say *"they can't be autistic, they know how to do y."* Understand that your child's diagnosis is surprising to you, and that's okay. I promise that you'll work through those feelings and after the diagnosis will come with more understanding and less confusion.

This Isn't What You Planned/Imagined

I remember my pregnancy and delivery with my son vividly. I went into labor six weeks too early and had a traumatic emergency cesarean. I didn't see him in person for about twelve hours after he was born. I remember spending much of my labor and delivery saying, *"but this isn't what was supposed to happen"*. I was supposed to have six more weeks. I was supposed to have a normal and simple delivery and then snuggle my son the second he was born. I never thought I would have a surgery and a two week NICU stay that included my newborn in a medically induced coma.

But see, that's all a part of life. Just like our labor and delivery stories are not always as we planned and imagined them to be, our children won't always be either. When you pictured your family, you may have seen being married by 25 and having two kids, a boy and a girl, by age 30. Maybe you always thought you'd be a teacher, but you've become a stay at home mom. Our lives are everevolving and the important thing to remember is that just because something isn't the way we imagined, it doesn't mean it's *worse* than our imagined realities.

When you were expecting, you probably spent hours thinking about what your child might be like. Maybe you had the perfect image of them at their preschool orientation, impressing their teacher with their knowledge of the ABC's. Maybe you dreamed of an elementary school concert where they'd joyfully, albeit off tune, sing their heart out with all of their friends. From playdates at the park, to snuggly "*I Love You's*" when they're sleepy, I'm betting you dreamed about your child's whole life. And if you're like most people, autism wasn't a part of that daydream. For most people, autism isn't even on their radar.

Feel free to take some time to acknowledge your feelings of what you thought your life with your child would be. I understand it can be disheartening when you feel like all of those dreams you had for your child are gone. Take your time to feel sad about that. But then remember that not everything will change, and that autism isn't a death sentence for your dreams. We'll chat more in the next few chapters about staying positive, I promise, but for now I want you to know that it's okay to feel sad about what you thought your life and your child's life would be like.

Your Life Will Be Different

It's a simple fact that your life will be different now autism is part of the picture. Expectations will need to be adjusted, but autism isn't necessarily going to disrupt your entire life, certain aspects may just look a little different from now on. You'll have therapies to go to, extra appointments with specialists and teachers, and more. But I promise that you'll get used to your "new normal" and this overwhelmed feeling will go away (mostly) eventually.

Some of the changes you may be facing immediately. Maybe you are starting a new therapy and you need to rearrange your schedule to make it work. Others may be changes down the road, like being prepared to fight for accommodations at your child's school or trying to help your child make friends.

Try not to get too far ahead of yourself. Take each day as it comes.

Learn all that you can about how to manage common struggles that you may be facing right now. Learn about your child's triggers and how to avoid potential meltdowns. Learn how to manage meltdowns when they inevitably happen.

Tackle any critical issues like safety in parking lots or physical aggression. Once you have those immediate concerns managed, you can start to adjust to the other changes you'll be facing.

The Future Can Be Scary

I know that you probably have ten million doctors, therapists, well-meaning family members, and more, telling you what to expect in the future. You might hear that your child won't ever talk or that they'll definitely struggle in high school. The fact is, no one knows where your child will be in the future. Autism is a huge spectrum, and there are millions of different "outcomes" possible. Children who were thought to have the intelligence of a toddler turned out to be geniuses when they learned to communicate through an iPad. Adults who would "never amount to anything" are starting crazy successful companies based on their interests and strengths. Autistic people who, twenty years ago, may have been unable to speak now have tons of devices available to them to make their voices heard. There's now a non-speaking autistic young woman hosting a talk show.

Our world is changing, technology is changing. No one can predict the future. Especially when it comes to your child.

Bottom line? I know that the future can be really scary. But just know that no one knows the future. Your child may never talk, your child may never make eye contact, your child may never graduate high school. Or your child may become a total chatterbox once they find a topic they want to talk about, your child may find other, more comfortable, ways to show they're paying attention than eye contact. Or your child may get a PHD or start a successful business. We won't know until it happens. Try not to let your idea of your child's future limit them. Don't assume your child can't do something. Work with your child to find the perfect balance of challenge and comfort.

Don't Panic Yet

When you get an autism diagnosis for your child, I know that it can be pretty panic inducing. You feel like you need to learn all the things at once and your child will always need more than you can do. Take a deep breath and remember that you are your child's parent for a reason. No one will advocate for your child like you will. No one can connect with your child like you can. I know how hard it is. I know it's scary. But remember that this is your child. This is the same child you brought home from the hospital as a tiny baby. It's the same child you woke up in the middle of the night to comfort. This diagnosis might seem like it's changed your entire life, but it has not changed your child.

There will be plenty of time to panic. But for now, take a moment, breathe deep, and enjoy the moment with your child.

Advocate Highlight: **Carly Fleischmann**

Carly Fleischmann is a non-speaking autistic self-advocate, author, and talk show host. Carly uses a ipad to type and communicate with those around her, and the girl is absolutely hilarious. She's had guests on her talk show, Speechless, such as Channing Tatum and James Van Der Beek. She also wrote and recorded a song, Glamour Girl, with Kaitlin Kozell and Lil Jaxe.
You can learn more about Carly at *CarlysVoice.com*

Chapter 4
Focusing on the Positives for Your Child

All right, friends, we're going to get back to that balance I mentioned in the last chapter. While it is okay to feel sad, or however you feel, you still need to do your best to stay positive around your child. See, your attitude and actions regarding your child's autism will stick with them, whether you think they notice or not. Kids are extremely perceptive, and it's important that they know that you love them just as much today as you did the day before their diagnosis.

In this chapter we'll chat about the different ways that your attitude can affect your child, and how to make sure we stay positive and help our child process their diagnosis while we're processing as well. Like before, it's all about a balance, and no parent gets it 100% right. Do your best, read the chapter, and really just try to be intentional about your own behaviors surrounding your child's new diagnosis.

Think About How Your Attitude Affects Your Child

Getting an autism diagnosis can be overwhelming and scary. You do your best to make it through the day. To make it through the next specialist appointment. To make it through the next evaluation. The last thing you want is another thing to think about, but I'm going to give you just this one thing, think for a minute about how your attitude surrounding the autism diagnosis is going to affect your child.

If you're visibly upset about your child's diagnosis, they'll have no choice but to be upset about it too. Our words and actions during this time can either bring our children's self-esteem up or tear it down, and that's a huge responsibility. It's okay to feel sad after getting your child's diagnosis, but keep it away from your child as much as possible.

When you are in the right mindset, you need to talk with your child. Explain to your child what autism is, how their brain works differently than other kids, and that some of their behaviors that they've been taught are "bad" aren't their fault. Have a conversation about what really cool things autistic people can do that neurotypical people struggle with, and talk about how things will hopefully get much easier now that you understand their brain more and can get help.

If you try your hardest to distance your child from their diagnosis, they will start to believe that there is something wrong with being autistic. That there is something wrong with who they are. You want your child to understand that your feelings about them haven't changed since they got a diagnosis. They need to know that you love them today just like you loved them last week and last year. Sure, you can be honest that they will face struggles, but give them the confidence that you will face those struggles together and you will always be on their side.

While this diagnosis has rocked your world, it's important to remember that this isn't actually about you. This is about your child. Yes, your parenting life may be harder than you originally thought it would be, but your child's life should be the focus as much as possible.

Now, I'm not saying you have to be 100% happy-go-lucky all the time. I understand the shock to your system when getting a diagnosis. Especially when you listen to the doctors go on and on about your child's deficits. By all means, call your best friend and cry on the phone. Have a late night chat with your spouse about your fears. Be honest with your child about struggles that the two of you may face together and how you plan on tackling those challenges. But always try to stay positive for your child.

Even If They "Can't Understand" They Do

I've heard this one more times than I can count. See, my son A-Man is considered high-functioning because he's verbal, and I'm considered highfunctioning because no one even knew I was autistic until I was in my midtwenties. I've often been criticized as not truly understanding the "severe end" of the spectrum. *"I don't have to stay positive around my child because they'll never understand what I'm saying anyways,"* is a phrase that I've heard often.

Here's the thing. Non-verbal does not mean non-intelligent. Non-verbal does not mean they have no understanding of the world around them. Thirty years ago, non-speaking autistics were assumed to have no cognitive understanding whatsoever. Now? There's a non-speaking autistic girl named Carly who hosts a talk-show. We now have more adaptive technologies than ever, and nonspeaking autistics are able to communicate with us in ways that were never possible before. We're now learning that those autistic people who *"had no idea what was happening"* definitely knew what was happening, they just didn't have the ability to communicate that understanding.

So why should you listen to high-functioning self-advocates even if you don't think your child will ever be like us? Because level of "functioning" changes. We have no idea what technologies and therapies will become available in the next twenty years that could allow your child to overcome barriers and achieve new levels of function. It's always the best bet to assume competence with your children. Assume that they are or will be capable of most things, including understanding you.

With that said, even if there are no new technologies over the next few decades that would benefit your child and your child never learns to speak or respond to you the way you would expect, they still feed off of your emotions. When you are sad, your child knows. Whether they can verbalize it or not, they will respond to that energy. How do I know this? Because you can watch your child's emotions change with your own. So, even if your child can't understand the words you're using, they can comprehend the emotions and energy that you're giving off.

The Problem With "Love the Child, Hate the Autism"

Something else I've heard often is that a parent *"loves their child but hates their autism."* Can I just get real for a second? This is one of the most harmful things a parent could say to, about, or around their child. Of course your child is a whole person, but autism is a part of who they are. Think about how many things your child does that are because of their autism. For my son, if he wasn't autistic he wouldn't stim when he gets excited. He wouldn't recite movie lines to communicate new feelings. He wouldn't need deep squeezes like he does now when he gets overwhelmed. Simply put, he wouldn't be the same A-Man that we know and love.

When parents' divorce, experts warn them to never talk negatively about the other parent in front of the children. The reasoning is simple, your child is half you and half the other parent. If you think the other parent is horrible, kids can internalize that to mean you think that half of them is horrible. Autism isn't really any different. Autism changes every part of your child's neurology, which changes every part of your child's personality, likes, dislikes, fears, comforts, and more. You can't hate something that is that big a part of your child without hating your child as well.

Help Your Child Embrace Their Autism

This can be the most difficult part of the journey towards embracing autism if you're still struggling to accept the diagnosis yourself, but it's wildly important. It is vital to talk to your child about their autism diagnosis. You will want to cover things like: What does it mean to be autistic? Who that they might know about was also autistic? What historical figures were autistic, and how did their autism help them succeed?

As you move on from that, and as your child matures, start to tell them about the autistic culture. Read books, blog posts, or listen to some podcasts or interviews done by autistic adults. Teach your child about the disability movement and the neurodiversity movement, and how autistic self-advocates have come so far over the last few decades to fight for autistic people to have the same rights as everyone else. Your child is going to need a community, a place of belonging, start bringing that world to them as they are ready.

Being autistic isn't a curse, it's truly just a difference. Helping your child identify their unique gifts that come with their autism will go a long way in helping both you and your child embrace their autism, and helping them truly start to feel proud to be autistic. Every autistic person's gifts will be unique, just like every neurotypical person's gifts are unique. Maybe your child has perfect pitch because of their sensitivity to sound. Maybe they're a math or piano prodigy. Maybe they're quite the comedian because of their super unique sense of humor. Whatever your child's particular gifts are, make sure that they're talked about just as much, if not more, than their struggles. Remember that your child's therapists, doctors, and evaluators will heavily focus on deficits. It's up to you, and your child, to focus on and embrace their strengths.

Advocate Highlight: **Benjamin K.M. Kellogg**

Benjamin K.M. Kellogg is a freelance writer, author, and autistic self-advocate. He wrote a children's book series, *Noah and Logan*, to help teach autistic children various social and life skills that they may struggle with. He's previously written an online column about his life as an autistic adult. You can find more information about Benjamin at *BenjaminKMKellogg.com*

Chapter 5
The Many Benefits of Autism

When we left A-Man's doctor's office with an official diagnosis, she was genuinely shocked that we weren't upset. She asked repeatedly how we were feeling and if we had any concerns. We didn't. We were prepared to get a diagnosis, though we thought it would take a bit longer. We had researched autism to death. We knew what we were facing with A-Man, we just had to wait for the right person to tell us.

On the way home I remember thinking about how his doctor's demeanor changed once she officially said that he was on the spectrum. It was as if she expected us to break down, and I simply couldn't understand it. Why do people get so upset hearing that their child is autistic? Don't they realize that while, yes, there are very real struggles, there are also benefits and wonders that make this whole journey worthwhile?

In this chapter we're going to unpack some of the benefits to autism. I know that if you're working your way through this book for the first time, and your child's diagnosis was recent you might be struggling right now. Take heart and know that in time you'll see the benefits more clearly than you do now. You'll be able to respond with positivity when someone tells you they're sorry that your child is autistic. This will likely become one of your favorite chapters if you take it to heart and give it some time.

Autistic People Are Different, Not Worse

While it can be a bit scary to get the initial diagnosis, it's important to know that autistic people are different from neurotypical people, but that does not mean we're worse. Just like men and women are different, but neither is worse. Understanding this will be key in starting to truly understand how to accept, understand, and advocate for your autistic child.

When you understand that autism is a neurological difference and not something to be cured or fixed, you'll be more likely to help your child grow up to be exactly who they should be. You'll choose therapies that help them learn coping strategies instead of therapies that aim to make them act neurotypical. You will be able to stand up against bullies and ableists who make negative remarks about your child or autism in general. This section is one of the most important in the entire book.

But how do we get past our preconceived notions about autism? It isn't always easy. Especially if you've had little experience with autistic people, or worse, you've only had negative experiences. Taking some time to learn about what autistic people face can be incredibly helpful.

When we think through our typical day, we can expect to face various discomforts and inconveniences. Think for a moment, though, about facing those same annoyances, except they are downright painful. The annoying lights at the office that give you a minor headache? For your child they are unbelievably painful, to the point where they may struggle to function. The line at the grocery store that's a little too long and has you picking at your nails or flipping through a magazine? It's going to have your child stimming and getting overstimulated.

Once you have a real understanding of what your child is going through, you have a lot more empathy and understanding when working with them. You will start to see that the issue isn't the fact that your child stims, it's the way that strangers judge them for stimming. It isn't a bad thing that your child likes quiet time to focus on their activities, it's bad that this go-go-go world doesn't give them time to fully explore their interests. Autistic brains work differently than neurotypical brains, but our brains are not broken or less.

Autistic People Have Different Strengths

Doctors and other autism professionals tend to spend a

lot of time focusing on deficits. They may go on and on about whether or not your child will ever talk, or the different physical struggles that your child may face. They'll explain all about your child's social struggles and they might even tell you your child won't ever make any friends. Here's the thing, those doctors don't have any idea what your child will be capable of in five years. More importantly, even if your child has all of the struggles that your doctor warns you of, they will still have strengths.

My sister is an incredible artist. She always has been. Drawing, painting, and even interior design and decorating cupcakes, she has always had an eye for the creative arts. Me? I draw stick figures and I never know what colors should go together, but I love writing. I've been writing since I was young, and I don't plan on stopping, whereas my sister could really care less about writing. We have different strengths.

Your child might be the next Picasso, or your child might have an incredible knack for computer games. Your child might excel in math, or maybe they can make amazing Lego builds. Maybe your child loves to dance and sing, maybe they love to draw. Maybe your child can make anyone in the world smile. Whatever your child's individual strengths, celebrate them and support your child in pursuing those strengths.

Autistic People See the World Differently

This is one of the hidden benefits to autism that people don't immediately understand. When our family goes for walks by the water, all of our kids get excited. They will stop and look to see if there are any fish or boats, and if not, they're ready to walk a bit more. A-Man? He will sit and watch the water for hours. Even if it's just the waves crashing onto the beach, the same way over and over again, he is absolutely fascinated.

When our other kids watch a movie, they remember the main story. A-Man can recite the most boring scenes. His attention to detail is absolutely incredible, but it would also be easy to miss if you didn't really pay attention to him.

Autistic people tend to see the world in much more detail than neurotypical people do. We also tend to be highly logical which can be seen as a benefit or a negative. Often our logical thoughts are seen as a deficit because we don't easily understand sarcasm. I see it as a benefit because I can often look through the emotions and find a logical solution to something that a group is struggling with.

In reality, many of autism's deficits can be reframed as benefits when you change your perspective. When you start looking at autistic people's behaviors as ways for us to more easily cope with society, instead of seeing our behaviors as ways that we're disrupting society, you can see that the behaviors aren't really negative at all.

Advocate Highlight: **Dr. Temple Grandin**

Dr. Temple Grandin is an autistic self-advocate, author, public speaker, scientist, and more. She didn't speak until she was 3.5 years old, and she was teased and bullied in school for being different. When she found her passion in science, she excelled. Dr. Temple Grandin was one of the first self-advocates to give a peek into the way autistic brains worked, and she's done incredible work for the autistic community. You can find more about Dr. Temple Grandin at *TempleGrandin.com*

Chapter 6

Understanding Autism Meltdowns and How to Handle Them

I have never been one to have babysitters often, but even more so once A-Man became a toddler. It seemed like if any tiny thing didn't go perfectly his way, he would lose his mind. If someone handed him the wrong snack, he would spend an hour screaming and be completely inconsolable. He also had troubles with language, and struggled to tell us what was wrong. We had to become mind-readers, and oftentimes it felt like we were walking on egg shells in our own home.

This, friends, is what living with meltdowns is like. Before we had A-Man's diagnosis, we mislabeled them tantrums. I would tell people *"I've never in my life seen a kid that can throw a fit like A-Man."* Turns out that his "fits" were truly autism meltdowns and he couldn't control them any more than I could. Thankfully I've learned plenty about meltdowns in the last few years, including how to recognize my own.

What in the World is a Meltdown?

An autism meltdown is when an autistic person loses control of themselves. Different autistic people meltdown in different ways. Some scream and cry, others act out with aggression, some self-harm, and still others shut down internally and become non-verbal for a period of time. A-Man tends to scream and cry or act out with aggression, while I tend to stim a lot and shut down internally when I have a meltdown.

Meltdowns happen when an autistic person is overwhelmed, and they can typically be traced back to a specific trigger. For A-Man, food with certain textures is terrifying and sometimes even painful, so being handed the wrong snack would definitely trigger a meltdown. For me, being touched in certain ways results in an immediate meltdown.

The most important thing to keep in mind with meltdowns is that meltdowns are happening to your autistic child, not to you. I know that it can be really embarrassing when your child throws themselves to the floor in the middle of Target. I know that the screams can make you feel absolutely crazy. I suffer from chronic migraines, so learning to handle the constant screaming during A-Man's meltdowns was, and still is, quite the struggle in our house. I'm not trying to say that meltdowns aren't difficult for parents, it's just a huge shift in mentality to see that your child is having a hard time, not giving you a hard time.

It's easy to get frustrated when the trigger of a multiple-hour meltdown is something that seems so small. Once A-Man had a meltdown that lasted hours because I gave him his breakfast in the wrong bowl. I'm not kidding at all. I may or may not have called my husband (remember, we need a tribe!) crying. Because I couldn't understand why in the world was the color of the bowl so important? The thing is, for autistic people, and in particular autistic kids who haven't learned as many coping skills, something so small to you can be a huge deal to us.

When our entire life is overwhelming and chaotic, we cling to our specific routines and preferences as our only coping mechanism. Having the same meal, in the same colored bowl, every day, takes less of our energy, so we can spend that energy on the overwhelming act of asking for breakfast and handling the baby touching us in a way we don't like.

How to Prevent Meltdowns

One of the easiest ways to prevent a meltdown is to keep consistent routines. The struggle is that we cannot stay a slave to a routine 100% of the time, and we owe it to our autistic children to help safely and slowly expose them to changes in routine so that they can develop their coping skills. When trying to determine if a routine is one that should be challenged or upheld, I try to consider whether it's a reasonable routine. For example, as grown adults, my husband and I both get the same thing every time we go to our favorite restaurant. It would be foolish of me to expect A-Man to change his order just for the sake of changing.

On the flip side, A-Man used to have a routine with getting in the car that involved which car door he used, and which order he and all of his siblings got in the car. That routine wasn't a reasonable routine to keep up with because A-Man needed to have the coping skills to get in and out of different cars or with different groups of people. There are also days where he had to get in the car without all of his siblings. There are natural changes occurring around getting in the car, so that's a routine that we changed up regularly (and handled the meltdowns) for a while until A-Man had the coping skills to tolerate it.

Another simple way to prevent meltdowns is to manage transitions successfully. Transitions can be extremely difficult for autistic people. Our brains just get set in what we're doing and we don't process the activity change very well. There's anxiety of the unexpected and, of course, the change in routine. Learning a few transition strategies can make a world of difference for you and your autistic child. Try a visual schedule to show your child what's happening next in their day, and give plenty of warnings. A lot of parents have success with timers, and we've made huge progress with giving A-Man three step transitions: "Shoes, Car, Park" or "Nima's, Therapy, Lunch", for example. We've also found that giving A-Man a transition object, like a small toy that he can keep with him through several transitions, has really helped. He feels safer knowing that he has one constant throughout the changes around him.

How to Handle a Meltdown When it's Happening

The first thing I want you to do during your child's next meltdown is to take a breath and remember that your child is not doing this on purpose. Even if your child is hurling insults or even fists at you, remember that this is not something your child is in control over. Oftentimes A-Man doesn't even remember what happens during his meltdowns because his fight or flight response completely takes over. Once you're in a calm-ish state of mind and feel ready to be there for your child, you can start helping your child manage their meltdown.

Of course, your first priority during your child's meltdown will be safety. Your child's, your own, and anyone around the two of you. Some families find it helpful to set up a safe place and a plan for what the siblings should do when your autistic child has a meltdown and loses control. If your autistic child selfharms during meltdowns, learn some safe techniques for using gentle restraints if necessary, and discuss with your child's doctors and therapists a safety plan for when you're at home managing a meltdown.

Beyond safety, there are certain ways that you can help your child through a meltdown that can help lower the time spent in the meltdown and help foster a more rapid recovery. As hard as it is, don't try to talk to your child. Once an autistic person is in a full-blown meltdown, we often won't be able to process what you're saying, and the extra input will only add to our sense of being overwhelmed. It's also a good idea to avoid eye contact, and in some cases even avoid looking face-to-face since our facial expressions can provide so much input for autistic children.

Know whether your child is a sensory seeker or sensory avoider, and help them find safe activities that give them the input that they need. For A-Man, he often needs deep squeezes or proprioceptive input from hitting something. For some autistic people, any sort of touch during a meltdown will only make it worse, so it's very important to know your child. Ask your child's therapist (our OT has been wonderful for this!) for specific advice on how to best meet your child's sensory needs during a meltdown.

Advocate Highlight: **John Elder Robison**

John Elder Robison is an autistic self-advocate and author of four books: *Look Me in the Eye*, *Be Different*, *Raising Cubby*, and *Switched On*. Growing up in the 60's, Asperger's was not yet a highly recognized diagnosis, so John learned about his Asperger's as an adult. Since then, he has become a fierce advocate and is currently a part of the Interagency Autism Coordinating Committee. This agency develops a strategic plan for autism research that guides NIH, CDC, and many private researchers. You can learn more about John at *JohnRobison.com*

Chapter 7
Fighting and Advocating for Autistics

I've already shared my story, how we struggled to get a referral for A-man. How the doctor ignored our concerns. How we had to fight to get the help we needed. As a parent of an autistic child, you need to be ready to fight and advocate for your child. It's not always going to be easy, but preparation will help you navigate the hurdles.

For some, advocating may be a new term that you're not used to. In a sense, it means to fight for your child to get access to the things that they need. You can advocate for accommodations in school or at work, advocate for accessibility in public parks, and more.

Advocating for Accommodations

There's a lot to know about accommodations. The thing is, autistic children have a right to reasonable accommodations, in school and in society at large, but it isn't always easy to convince others of that fact. You should be ready to fight for the accommodations that your child needs and deserves.

To advocate for accommodations, you have to know what types of accommodations are available, helpful, and reasonable. Accommodations can be absolutely anything that help your child live their life more comfortably in everyday society. Some children require fidgets to help them stay calm and focused. Other children need the ability to move while they listen to something. A-Man needs extra time to process directions, and he needs repeated warnings before a transition. As an autistic adult, I still need accommodations like an item to fidget with when I need to focus.

The most important part of advocating for

accommodations for your child is that you know what accommodations are reasonable to expect. It is perfectly okay to expect your child's school to give them more time on their homework if that's what they need. You are not being "*that mom*" if you fight so that your child is included in the Lego club that they're dying to try, even if it means that the Lego club needs to be understanding of your child's autism and the way it might make them act differently than other children in the program.

Advocating for Understanding

It's one thing to get someone to agree to meet your accommodation expectations, but it's another to get true understanding for your child. Think about it for a second, it has taken a while for you to truly understand your child and their quirks, so it will take a while for others, who aren't as close to your child, to reach a similar level.

It's one thing for your child's teacher to be aware of autism. At this point, almost everyone is aware. They know that autism is a thing, and lots of kids have it, and it makes them "act weird".

It's an entirely different scenario when someone actually understands autism. Someone who understands, won't think twice when your child doesn't look them in the eye when they're talking. Someone who understands, won't be concerned when your child starts stimming.

I've noticed that it helps when talking to people about autism, to point out the similarities or parallels to some traditionally autistic behaviors. For example, many autistic people fidget while they're trying to stay focused, but many neurotypical people tap a pencil or chew their fingernails in the exact same scenario. When an autistic person faces sensory overload, I've compared that to being starving while you have a migraine, and then having to face the grocery store. It's not fun, and even the littlest thing becomes painful and unbearable. Drawing these parallels helps neurotypical people to understand and accept typical autistic traits.

Fighting for understanding is going to be an on-going battle. A-Man got his diagnosis two years ago, and we're still working on building understanding in some close friends and family. And I get it! Autism is a big thing, and it can be hard for anyone to fully process and understand. Not to mention it's such a huge spectrum, so a teacher who understands A-Man's autism wouldn't necessarily understand someone else's autism.

I want to encourage you to keep advocating. Keep explaining autism, even when you're getting eye rolls. Keep explaining why your child does what they do. When you help promote understanding of autism, you are helping not just your child, but every person in the autistic community.

Advocating for Acceptance

This will likely be the most difficult fight that you'll face after getting your child's autism diagnosis, and this fight starts with you. Buying this book was already a huge step towards winning this fight, and once you've won it yourself, you can help others to reach acceptance. See, truly accepting your child's autism is a huge step. It means that not only do you understand why they're stimming, but you think it's perfectly okay that they're stimming. You go beyond understanding that autism makes eye contact difficult and often times painful, and you stop trying to force eye contact.

With those outside of your immediate family, this acceptance can look different. When talking to children, I first help them understand what autism is and how it changes the way that A-Man acts, communicates, and plays. Then I spend time talking about how A-Man is different, but not bad. We talk about how A-Man's autism helps him to remember all the words to the latest kid's movie, and other ways that it makes him a totally awesome friend.

For adults, accepting autism can be more difficult than it is for children. See, we adults grew up in a different world. Kids were kids, and they were expected to listen to adults and behave. Our parents didn't read books about how to best understand and respect us, they expected us to understand and respect them. When a child moved a lot, they were considered too hyper, they weren't taken to a therapist to evaluate how to best support their sensory system. Nowadays, our world has begun to center around acceptance.

Helping adults accept autism can be as simple as directly pointing out internal biases that people may not even be aware that they have. When someone gets frustrated with A-Man's stimming, I ask them directly *"what is it hurting?"* They never have an answer beyond it being *"weird."* When someone says that autistic kids should be allowed in mainstream classrooms *"unless they're a disruption,"* I question how an autistic child's disruption that is out of their control is any worse than a neurotypical child's disruption because they're bored?

Advocate Highlight: Dani Bowman

Dani Bowman is an autistic advocate, public speaker, and founder of her own animation company, *DaniMation Entertainment*. DaniMation Entertainment employs autistic musicians, artists, and voice actors, and Dani leads summer animation camps around the country. Dani speaks regularly about autism and the need for self-sufficiency and employment for people with disabilities.
You can find more about Dani at *DaniBowman.com*

Chapter 8
Everything You Really Need to Know About Functioning Labels

One of my best friends has an autistic daughter. Since most of our mom friends don't understand autism, we often chat with each other about our autistic kids. One of the things we've talked about often is how our two children have been labeled on the functioning scale, and how pointless those labels are.

See, her daughter is a teenager that does not verbally communicate and will likely need support through her adult life. Because of this, she is considered lowfunctioning. My son is 6, he does verbally communicate, and we have no idea what types of supports he will need as he ages. Primarily based on the fact that he can communicate verbally, many would consider him high functioning.

What's the issue with that? Well, for one, it only takes one section of the autism spectrum into account. My friend's daughter is extremely sociable, and has no problem making friends. She's gentle and kind, and loves to be around people. My son struggles with aggression, especially around new people. During one meltdown where he lost control, he attempted to head butt his baby sister and would have done some serious damage if I hadn't caught him before he made contact. Why, then, is my son considered high functioning while her daughter, who's never hurt anyone, considered low functioning?

What are Functioning Labels

Functioning labels are, in theory, a simple way to describe where a person may fall on the autism spectrum. The labels break the spectrum up into two major categories, *"high functioning"* and *"low functioning"*. A high functioning autistic, again in theory, is a person who has autism that doesn't significantly impact their ability to function in everyday life. A low functioning autistic, by contrast, is a person who has autism that does significantly impact their ability to function in everyday life.

Typically, high functioning is representative of an autistic person who can verbally communicate, can meet educational milestones, and/or does not appear to need significant support in everyday life. On the flip side, low functioning is typically representative of an autistic person who is non-speaking, does not meet educational milestones, and/or needs significant support in everyday life. Functioning labels are often used to determine the need for accommodations, and they are supposed to help parents and professionals get on the same page with their expectations of an autistic person's future and abilities.

The Issue With Functioning Labels

The biggest issue that I have with functioning labels is that they're simply not very accurate. They show a misunderstanding of the autism spectrum in general (we'll get more to that in the next section) and they can be damaging to autistic people.

See, when a parent hears that their child is low functioning, they often set much lower expectations. The school district may decide not to challenge a child, claiming *"well we didn't really expect her to talk, she's low functioning"*. On the flip side, when a parent hears that their child is high functioning they can create unrealistic expectations of their child to "act normal" in situations that their child can't cope in a neurotypical way. If they have extreme anxiety with social situations, their parents may believe they just aren't trying hard enough.

Beyond this, there's a big disparity in what abilities truly determine a person's ability to *"function"*. If an autistic person can drive, they're high functioning, but if their social anxiety is so severe that they can't leave the house without a caregiver or aid, do they really function better than an autistic person who can't drive but thrives taking public transportation around town?

Looking back to the story of my son and my friend's daughter. Is my son really more able to function than her daughter because he can use movie scripts to speak, but he goes into extreme rages and my friend's daughter doesn't speak but can communicate lovingly?

The Autism Spectrum is Not a Straight Line

A lot of people look at the autism spectrum almost like a timeline. They believe it goes from a little autistic to very autistic, and each autistic person falls somewhere on that line. The issue is, that's not how the autism spectrum works. Not all autistic people have the same strengths and struggles. An autistic person can have significant struggles with verbal communication, but have very few sensory difficulties and vice-versa.

In reality, the spectrum has different sections like social development, sensory struggles, and executive functioning. A person can be effected by their autism in any combination of the sections, and each of those sections can have varying degrees of severity. Once I found this type of representation of the spectrum, it became so much easier for me to visualize and understand the true autism spectrum.

There's a common saying that when you've met one person with autism, you've met **one** person with autism, and that's really true. Each autistic person's struggles and strengths will vary, just like every neurotypical person's struggles and strengths will vary. When we talk about autism in terms of functioning labels, we leave out any room for understanding the person as an individual.

How Functioning Labels Lead to Dividing the Autism Community

A lot of time is devoted in this book to talking about the divide in the autism community between autistic people and parents of autistic children. Beyond that divide, there's a huge divide when it comes to these functioning labels. There is a common misconception that neurodiversity advocates are only high functioning autistics, and that we can't truly understand the struggle that low functioning autistics (and by extension, their parents) face. To any of you who feel like accepting and embracing autism are just thoughts for people with high functioning autism, please do some research on Carly Fleischmann. She's a nonspeaking autistic self-advocate who helps run the Autistic Self Advocacy Network and hosts her own talk-show.

If I had a dollar for every time someone told me that I don't understand *real autism*," I would be a rich, rich lady. I've even been criticized for writing books like this one because my son and I are both considered "*high functioning*" and that means that I don't understand what it really means to be autistic. Let me take a second to tell you that this is garbage. Functioning labels do not define "*how autistic*" you are, and as we chatted about before, they're extremely inaccurate.

Functioning labels give professionals and parents of autistic children a reason to separate themselves from autistic self-advocates, and it's a practice that needs to stop. Even if your child is non-speaking, even if your child has incontinence struggles, even if your child has violent aggressive meltdowns, they still deserve the dignity and respect that autistic self-advocates fight for. Whether you see your child as low or high functioning, let them live up to their potential and try not to keep them in a box of what you and the "*experts*" expect them to be able to do.

Advocate Highlight: **Dr. John Hall**

Dr. John Hall is an Autistic author, public speaker, and cofounder of the education tech company Greenwood & Hall. Diagnosed as *"severely autistic"* and *"slightly mentally retarded"* as a toddler by several doctors, his parents were told it would be impossible for him to live a normal life and that he would end up in a group home. His mother advocated fiercely for him, and he went on to have a mainstream education, run a successful business, and write his book, *"Am I Still Autistic?"*

Chapter 9
Evaluating Autism Organizations

When I first learned about A-Man's autism, I went into full research mode. I was reading books and blog posts, watching videos, participating in forums, and more. I was going to be the best autism mom there ever was.

So, naturally, my first instinct was to find and cling to the autism awareness campaigns that I saw all over social media. That blue puzzle piece sure is tempting, isn't it? I loved my autistic son, and I wanted to let the entire world know how proud I was of him.

Then I learned a bit more about that blue puzzle piece and what it represented. What I found wasn't pretty. Sexism, ableism, promises of "*cures*" and more... I knew that wasn't something I wanted to be a part of, so I started to dig a bit deeper.

But how do we know which organizations actually understand, accept, and embrace autism? In this chapter we're going to dig into some of that research and learn how to evaluate different autism organizations.

What to Look for in an Autism Organization

When I learn about an autism organization, there are a few key things that I look for before giving them my support. It's important to know that no group, non-profit, or organization will be absolutely perfect. Take some time to evaluate several organizations and find one that ties in most closely with your values.

First, I look at whether or not the organization has any autistic members on their board. This may not seem like a huge deal, but it's one of the biggest factors I use to decide whether an autism organization is worthy of my support. As an autistic self-advocate, it's important to me that any autism organization I support values the opinions of autistics, rather than only listening to the voices of parents or specialists.

The next thing that I consider when evaluating autism organizations is where their money goes. I was devastated to learn that one of the most popular autism organizations in the United States allocates only 4% of their budget to help autistic people or their families with their family grants. Look at the programs that the group runs and evaluate how each program actually helps autistic people before deciding to give your support.

Finally, I look at the beliefs and views that the autism organization is communicating about autism and disabilities in general. Do they respect the opinions of autistic self advocates? Do they support parents and families of autistic people while still embracing the autistic community? Do they present autism as an "*epidemic*" or a disease that people should fear? Consider these questions as you move forward in your research.

As a reminder, there is no perfect autism organization. Not one. At the end of this chapter I'll share a few of the autism organizations I tend to support, but each of them has its own positives and negatives. Do your own research and find the organization that fits closely to your values.

What to Avoid in an Autism Organization

When an autism organization says that a large portion of their funding goes towards "*research*", my spidey senses start tingling. There isn't anything inherently wrong with autism research, but it's vital that we look into what exactly the group is researching. I avoid any organization that supports cure-based research or research into prenatal diagnosis processes for autism. I cannot support any one that believes autistic people should not exist as we are.

Another thing I tend to avoid in autism organizations

is too much of a parent focus. It's wonderful to help support parents who are learning more about how to help and advocate for their autistic child, but the focus should be primarily on helping autistic people. Helping parents learn to advocate and accommodate for their children are great. Focusing on giving parents an avenue to control their autistic children or restrict their children's rights isn't.

It also goes almost without saying, I would avoid any organization that uses ableist language or presents ableist attitudes in its marketing. If any autism group gives you a bad feeling, skip it. There are some wonderful organizations that you can give support to without hesitation.

Autism Organizations to Support

The first autism organization I recommend giving your support is the Autistic Self Advocacy Network (ASAN). The ASAN's focus is on autistic self advocates, and their slogan is "*Nothing About Us Without Us*". Basically, the ASAN's position is that no decision should be made about autism resources or therapy without the input of autistic people. ASAN is an autism organization run by and for autistic people, and there are several autistic self-advocates on their board.

Another autism organization that's doing good work for autistic people is The Autism Project. While The Autism Project does focus more heavily on parents and families of autistics, their programs directly improve the lives of autistics. They provide social skills groups for autistic people of all ages, community events, and consultations to help families connect with their local programs available to them. The Autism Project has also collaborated with Hasbro on a project called Toybox Tools to make Hasbro toys more accessible to autistic children. The downside with The Autism Project is that they focus heavily on autistic children and don't have quite as many resources for autistic teens and adults.

Finally, I recommend checking out the Autism Women's Network (AWN). The primary goal of The Autism Women's Network is to dispel stereotypes and misinformation surrounding an autism diagnosis while building acceptance and understanding of disability. I appreciate that they have a nice blend of resources for parents and autistic girls and that they provide a safe space for female autistics who are so often drowned out in other organizations.

Advocate Highlight: **Alix Generous**

Alix Generous is an autistic mental health activist, public speaker, and writer. She's also an award winning scientist, and the cofounder of a biotech company called Autism Sees. Autism Sees produces an app that evaluates and helps develop social skills and can simulate job interview experiences for autistic people. In her Ted Talk, she describes having Aspergers as *"a pain in the butt and also a gift".*
You can find more about Alix at *AlixGenerous.com*

Chapter 10
Why and How to Listen to Autistic Self-Advocates

When you get your child's autism diagnosis, I'm sure the doctor will send you home with dozens of resources. You'll have phone numbers of therapists to call, flyers and pamphlets explaining exactly what autism is, fact sheets telling you what to expect, and more. The one thing they probably won't send you home with? Anything from autistic self-advocates.

See, our society still sees others as the experts on autism. Doctors, therapists, psychologists, and even parents are promoted as the voice for the autism community. That's a problem that needs to be addressed and fixed, and it's only going to be fixed if parents like you and I make a conscious effort to seek out and listen to autistic voices.

The Break in the Autism Community

I've talked a lot so far in this book about the Autism Community. The fact is, this community is huge and awesome, but there's a few pretty severe divides. One of the biggest, and most upsetting, divides is between autistic adults and parents of autistic children.

Note, this section is going to include several generalizations. There are definitely autistic adults that side with parents and parents that side with autistic adults. With that said, let's explore what this divide typically looks like in the autism community.

First, let's chat about autistic adults. I happen to be one, so I think I have some authority to give the general thoughts and beliefs we tend to have. First and foremost, the overwhelming majority of autistic adults are 100% okay with being autistic. We don't want a cure. We don't want sympathy. Quite simply, we are all about embracing autism. Beyond that, we feel that our autism is a huge part of our identity. We're autistic, just like we're men or women. Because of this, we tend to prefer "*identity language.*" The next chapter is going to be all about identity language, but for a basic overview, we prefer to say "*Sally is autistic*" versus "*Sally has autism*".

Now, parents tend to be on the opposite side on many of these issues. Many parents don't want to embrace their child's autism diagnosis, they grieve it. They search for a cure, and support organizations that are researching for that cure. They do want sympathy. They focus on how hard autism makes their lives, rather than seeing how autism has improved their children's lives. Because parents tend to want to distance their child from the autism, they prefer "*person-first language*" which is basically "*Joey has autism*" versus "*Joey is autistic*".

Why Autistic People Are the True Experts

With so many autism experts out there, it can be really difficult to know who to listen to. I mean, there are a million doctors and therapists giving you their professional opinions, there are a million mom-blogs like mine (*Autistic Mama*) that give you short tips and tricks. There are books like this one that share the author's perspective. Then there are autistic self-advocates sharing online and inperson. Everyone seems to be screaming for your attention and it can be hard to know who to listen to.

Please, please, please, listen to autistic adults. Above all else, autistic people are the true experts on autism. We experience it, and live it, every day. These autistic adults are your child grown up, so why wouldn't we listen to autistic self-advocates over others? When an autistic person tells you that a therapy is harmful and gave them PTSD, listen! When an autistic person says that they don't like the term "*special needs,*" listen!

Here's the thing, you're going to offend someone, but when given the choice wouldn't you rather offend someone outside of your child's community? A-Man isn't old enough to make his preferences on things like language or therapies clearly known yet, but I'd rather spend his childhood using the information that I have from people like him. What if I ignored autistic self-advocates, and always sided with parents and professionals? What would happen to my relationship with my son when he's older and becomes an adult self-advocate? I'd rather side with autistic people every time.

Also, as just a quick note, here's another place that some moms can say *"my child will never be a self-advocate because they're non-speaking/low functioning."* To that I say, please re-read the last chapter and every autistic self-advocate highlighted in this book. Even if you don't believe now that your child will become a self-advocate, it's really impossible to tell. Always. Assume. Competence.

How to Listen to Autistic People

It can seem difficult and overwhelming to figure out how to listen to autistic people. How can you easily find the general opinion of the autism community? It isn't like everyone has an autistic best friend that we can run everything by, and if you did they'd probably get annoyed. Thankfully, there are a few super simple ways to find, listen to, and respect the opinions of autistic adults.

First, check out the Autistic Self Advocacy Network (ASAN). It's an organization of autistic self-advocates, and their allies, that actually helps autistic people. They promote supports and therapies for autistic people, instead of funding research for a "cure" or prenatal autism screening. Their website and social media channels often release statements about current events that affect autistic people, and their opinions are often the general consensus of the autistic community at large.

You can also find information on several social media sites by searching the hashtag #actuallyautistic. I've found tons of awesome information on tumblr and reddit by searching that hashtag, and it can really help to find a community of people who are, well, actually autistic.

When there isn't a way to get a direct opinion from autistic adults, keep in mind the generality in the last section.

Autistic people want respect and understanding. In general, if what you're doing is respectful to autistic people, you're probably in the clear. In the next section we'll go through some of the common beliefs and opinions held by the autistic community at large.

What Autistic People Typically Have to Say

We already covered the language preferences, in that, we tend to prefer "*autistic.*" Another language preference that many autistic people have is against the cutesy names for disabilities like "*handicapable.*" Terms like that tend to infantilize autistic people. They can also make it seem like reasonable accommodations for autistic people are special treatment, when really they are just necessary changes to put everyone on a level playing field. Autistic people also often speak out against certain therapies. In particular ABA, or applied behavioral analysis, is routinely seen as a negative therapy.

Autistic people tend to prefer therapies that make life easier for autistic people, over therapies designed to make autistic people act neurotypical. A therapy that helps an autistic person learn to stay safe from self-harm during a meltdown? Totally fair game. A therapy that tries to stop autistic people from having meltdowns so that they don't embarrass their parents at the grocery store? Not so much.

The other main issue that autistic people advocate for is dignity, respect, and privacy for autistic people (and especially children). This tends to be where parents and self-advocates argue the most. It's become very popular in recent years for "autism moms" to share about their experiences, particularly online. This isn't a bad thing, necessarily, I mean, I'm a mom blogger, I totally understand writing about your life. What autistic people argue against is the oversharing of personal details that many parents are doing. It's very important to keep in mind that your child's autism is their story. They deserve the dignity and respect of sharing their story on their terms.

Now, this is a fine line. Because parents do need to hear from other parents. They need their tribe. So how do we share our story without overstepping? First and foremost, give your child some anonymity. There's a reason you'll see my son often referred to as A-Man. The other way to stop from overstepping is to remember to come at everything from a place of respect. Would you be comfortable with someone sharing the story if it was about you? If not, don't post. You won't ever see a video of my son mid-meltdown on my social media page because I wouldn't ever want someone to share that about me. Intimate medical details, meltdowns, bathroom habits and more, should be off-limits.

Again, if you want to stay on the side of autistic adults, come at everything you do from a place of respect. Know that your child is a person, first and foremost, and that there isn't anything "wrong" with them. Your child will eventually be an autistic adult, so learning to listen to autistic adults' preferences now is only going to help you in the long run.

Advocate Highlight: Darius Brown

Darius Brown is a 5th grade autistic self-advocate and published author. After being diagnosed autistic at 22 months old, he received speech and motor therapies, and has been in mainstream classes at his elementary school since kindergarten. He wrote a book, *Darius Hates Vegetables*, to help encourage kids to try vegetables at least once, even if they smell bad!
You can find more about Darius at *IAmDariusBrown.com*

Chapter 11
Understanding the Importance of Identity Language

There is another divide in the autism community that no one seems to agree on. Should we say "*autistic*?" Or should we say "*person with autism*?" Maybe it should be "on the autism spectrum." Or possibly even, as one person tried to tell me, "*a person who likes trains, is adventurous, and happens to have autism.*" Yes, by the way, someone really thought you needed at least two specific descriptions of the person before mentioning their autism.

This debate may seem a bit silly. Don't they all mean the same thing? Well, on the surface, all of these phrases mean that the person is autistic. However, each of them come with subtle differences that show underlying beliefs about autism. In this chapter we'll get into the nitty gritty of person-first and identity language and why this divide in the autism community exists.

What is Identity Language and Person-First Language

Identity language is language that includes autism as part of a person's identity. Examples of identity language include "*I am autistic,*" "*he is autistic,*" "*my daughter is autistic,*" etc. Identity language comes with the understanding that you have accepted and are embracing your autism, and you own it as a part of your personal culture. You could say "*my son is autistic*" like you would say "*my son is Hispanic.*"

Person-first language is language that attempts to separate the person from their autism in an effort to remind the world that the autistic person is, in fact, a person. It began being heavily promoted by the Down Syndrome community, since people with Down Syndrome were often not given basic human rights and dignity, so society needed that reminder that first and foremost they are people. When it became so widely accepted for the Down Syndrome community, many people adapted it for the disability community in general. Examples of person-first language include *"person with autism"* *"child on the autism spectrum"* *"a child who happens to have autism"* etc.

Why is Identity Language Preferred by Autistic People

Identity language tends to be preferred by autistic people because we see our autism as a part of our identity. We are autistic just like we are men or women. Just like we are students and brothers and mothers and sons. Just like we are black or white or Asian or French. It is a part of who we are, and we don't shy away from that. You would never say that your child *"happens to have brunetteness"*, you'd say he's a brunette. My husband doesn't "happen to have a physical competency that allows him to excel in sport-like activities" he is athletic. By that same token, I'm autistic. I'm a writer. I'm a mother. I'm a sister and daughter and friend. And I'm autistic. Separating a person from their autism is like separating a person from their ethnicity or gender. It just doesn't work.

Besides the fact that you can't really separate a person from their neurology, we don't really want you to try. We embrace our autism, and we don't feel the need to distance ourselves from it. When you try to separate your child from their autism with person-first language, you're subtly communicating to the world (and your child) that their autism is something to be upset or ashamed about. When you attempt to separate the person from their disability, you further the stigma that there's something wrong with disabilities.

Why is Person-First Language Preferred by Parents and Professionals

Parents of autistic children and autism professionals tend to prefer person-first language, even after they hear that autistic self-advocates prefer identity language. A lot of it stems from parents and experts seeing autism as a medical diagnosis and believing it's a negative thing. When you feel like your child was *"stolen"* by their autism, you want them to be distanced as far as possible from their diagnosis.

For others, the struggle is that they want the world to see their child as a person, not just hear the diagnosis and make assumptions. I totally understand this one. I get nervous that people will hear that A-Man is autistic and make snap judgements about him that aren't accurate and are hurtful. But here's the thing. If we try to shield society from our children's autism, we aren't moving society's judgements forward at all. When we try to hide the autism, society doesn't see all of the benefits to autism and the ways that your kiddo's autism makes them unique and wonderful.

Advocate Highlight: **Corinne Duyvis**

Corinne Duyvis is an autistic self-advocate and author who writes sci-fi novels featuring autistic main characters. She's the cofounder of Disability in Kidlit, an organization committed to reviewing and discussing the way disabilities are portrayed in middle grade and young adult literature. At age 14, Corinne was diagnosed with autism and dropped out of high school. By 19, she had graduated from art school and had started writing.
You can find more about Corinne at *CorinneDuyvis.com* and *DisabilityinKidlit.com*

Chapter 12
Remember, Autistics Have Joy

The other day we were at a barbecue at my sister's house. This is a regular event for us since we moved into a house with no yard. See, five kids trapped in a house without a place to play outside? It doesn't work well. Thankfully my sister lives five minutes away and we just hijack her yard whenever we get antsy! Anyways, regular family functions like this used to be incredibly difficult for A-Man. He couldn't tolerate the food. He got overwhelmed by my sister's pets. My nephew didn't understand A-Man and A-Man didn't understand my nephew, which lead to some serious cousin brawls.

Lately, though, we've been to my sister's enough to develop a sense of normalcy and comfort. A-Man knows to expect the animals and tolerates them well, as long as the big dog doesn't come too close to him. He starts saying *"Auntie Christy!"* when we turn the corner to her house. He's been getting along with my nephew, and my sister even keeps some frozen chicken nuggets on hand to make for him when he needs dinner. The last time we were there, A-Man was lying on the walkway, playing with cars. He wasn't talking to anyone, no one was talking to him. He was just playing with his cars and reciting scenes from the Cars movies. Pure joy. Any of my other kids would have been bored in minutes, but A-Man was just blissful for over an hour before we left.

What's the point in my story about seemingly nothing? That's just it. A-Man finds joy in the things that many people would never truly understand or appreciate. He gets overjoyed when he finds water anywhere. He thinks that tiny toy race cars are the best invention ever made. His face lights up when someone remembers he likes ketchup with his chicken nuggets. This kid has serious joy. During the diagnosis process and all of the therapies, often that joy gets overlooked. We focus on deficits and what your child may never do without acknowledging that your child is a person and they will have true joy.

Autistic People Experience Life

Autistic people have lives. Did you know that? We get married. We have friends. We have jobs. We go to prom (and it doesn't need to be newsworthy!) and we get dumped. Now again, this is where some parents of children who have more "*severe*" autism will say "*well my child won't do that.*" Here's the thing. Your child may not go to prom or have a job, but your child still has a life. They still feel the wind on their face when you walk outside. They can still feel the grass under their feet when they play at the park. Their life may look different than what you expected for them, but it is still a life.

Autistic people don't just experience life, but they can love life. In a supportive environment, autistic people can thrive. You're taking huge strides towards creating this supportive environment by reading this book and doing all that you can to fully embrace your child's autism diagnosis. Think about it. All people want to feel accepted and loved. When people have that safety net, they can explore the world around them and create their own life experiences with confidence. Autistic people are no different.

When you chat with an autistic person about life, you might be amazed at all of the things that you're currently taking for granted. Many autistic people have a heightened sense of awareness. That's part of what causes us to easily become overwhelmed and have meltdowns. On the flip side, though, it allows us to notice and appreciate things that many people gloss over. The video on Facebook you see of an autistic person drawing an entire city scape by memory? The same part of his brain that allows him to create that masterpiece is what may cause him to be overwhelmed by the sound of a bug buzzing near him.

Autistic People Will Have Friends

The assumption that autistic people will never have friends is one of the most hurtful and confusing to me. I didn't know I was autistic until my twenties, so naturally my friends didn't know either. I have always had friends, from a very early age. The way I relate to friends is different than neurotypical people, but that doesn't make them any less my friends. A-Man is decidedly less social than I was as a child, and he still makes friends.

When autistic people struggle to keep friends, the majority of the time it's because society lacks understanding and acceptance of typical autistic behaviors. Neurotypical children may not understand why their autistic friend is stimming or why they avoid eye contact. Simple education in the basics of autism would solve so many of the struggles with neurodiverse friendships.

That said, most autistic people will be able to find friends. Whether they find those friends within the autism community, at school, or in niche clubs they're involved in, there are plenty of opportunities for autistic children to make friends. In reality, it's typically parents that have a harder time with their child's friendships. They may try to force their kids to become friends with other kids that aren't a natural fit, or perhaps they're so convinced that no one will want to be their child's friend that they push friendships too heavily.

The best thing that you can do as a parent is to take a step back and let it happen. Offer natural explanations when warranted, for example, *"sometimes when A-Man is really excited he slaps his hands on his tummy and face. It's called 'stimming' and it makes him feel even happier!"* And simply allow your kids to find the friends that they naturally gravitate towards.

Advocate Highlight: Amythest Schaber

Amythest Schaber is an autistic writer, public speaker, advocate, and activist. They run a video series on youtube called "*Ask an Autistic*", and design t-shirts and prints that celebrate neurodiversity at Neurowonderful. Amythest was diagnosed autistic as an adult after autism burnout caused them to drop out of college and explore diagnosis possibilities.

You can learn more about Amythest at *neurowonderful.tumblr.com*

Chapter 13
Final Thoughts on Embracing Autism

When you got your child's autism diagnosis, it probably felt like your world was turned upside-down. When you picked names and dreamed about counting those tiny toes during your pregnancy, the last thing on your mind was therapy choices or identity language. I want to say that I'm proud of you for taking this step to do something different than most autism parents. By choosing to read this book, you've made a conscious choice to understand, accept, and embrace your child's autism, and that's something that few autism parents will ever do.

You are such a huge part of your child's life, and your acceptance will do worlds of good for your child's self-worth as they grow up. You are putting yourself in the best possible position to help your child develop into an autistic self-advocate that can rock their autism and fight alongside the autistic community for equal rights, accommodations, and accessibility.

I want you to know that you will have hard days. I embrace the heck out of my autism and A-Man's, but there are some days that are just plain hard. There are days where his needs and mine clash to an unbelievable degree, and it takes a world of patience to balance our own sensory needs. There are days where I have a migraine and as much as I know it isn't his fault, I just can't handle his screaming meltdown. I think we will always have those days, and you probably will to.

Simply by making the effort to understand your child's autism completely. To accept that they're autistic, and to embrace all that autism will throw at the both of you, you're worlds ahead in being able to have more successful days than hard days. I promise that the hard days get easier, and the successful days will become more frequent as time goes on. Like I've said throughout this book, you will always have challenges, and just when you get one challenge completely figured out it will change to a new challenge.

My hope is that with this book you will be armed to face those challenges. You will be ready to attack those challenges with your child as an ally instead of working against your child and viewing them as the challenge to be conquered.

Read this book over and over again when needed. Refer back to the chapters that really pull on your heart strings. Remember always that I'm rooting for you, and that you're an incredible parent. You're making great steps towards becoming a true autism advocate, and I'm proud of you!

Terms to Know and Further Reading

When you first get your child's autism diagnosis, or even if you've had the diagnosis for a while, there are a lot of new terms and a lot to learn. I wanted to take a moment at the end of this book to define a few terms and outline some further reading that can take you further on your journey to embracing autism.

First, I highly recommend that you join our private Facebook Community at *https://autisticmama.com/ea-community/* to connect with other parents, autistic selfadvocates, and more all joining together on our journeys toward embracing autism in our lives. This group is a safe space for autistic people and parents, and I know you'll find a home there.

I also recommend that you look for the following books to read, once you've finished this one: *Neurotribes* by Steve Silberman, *Look Me in the Eye* by John Elder Robison, *Uniquely Human* by Barry M. Prizant, and *The Reason I Jump* by Naoki Higashida. You can find my full recommended reading list at *https://autisticmama.com/ea-reading-list/*.

The following terms are used in this book or are commonly used in the autism community:

Functioning Labels - Labels that aim to describe the severity of a person's autism. These labels, such as "*high functioning*" and "*low functioning*" are outdated, inaccurate, and can be harmful to autistic people.

Identity Language - Language that includes autism as a part of a person's identity. "*She is autistic*"

IEP - Individualized Education Plan, a plan designed to outline a child's educational goals, accommodations, and expectations in the school system.

Meltdown - When an autistic person becomes overwhelmed and loses control of their behaviors.

Neurodivergent - A person whose neurology differs from the norm. This does not mean autistic, as it can include any neurological differences including giftedness and ADHD among others.

Neurodiversity - The understanding that everyone's neurology is naturally different, and those differences are a part of our natural world and necessary in society.

Neurodiversity Movement - A movement that embraces neurodiversity and fights for neurodivergent people to be understood and accepted by society as a whole.

Neurotypical - A person whose neurology is the norm or average. This does not mean not autistic, it means someone who is completely typical and doesn't have any difference from typical neurology.

Person-First Language - Language that separates a person from their autism. "She happens to have autism"

Stimming/Stims - Self-stimulating behavior. Often a repetitive behavior a person does when happy, excited, or overwhelmed. Flapping hands, tapping a pen, or repeating certain sounds are all examples of stims.

Acknowledgements

First and foremost, I would like to thank my partner, my advocate, and my biggest cheerleader: my husband, Chris. Thank you for the late night chats, the never-ending encouragement, and keeping our family running while I hid away with my laptop.

Next, of course I'd love to thank my kids. We've been through a lot since I started writing this book, and you all have handled the transitions beautifully. Thank you for giving me endless inspiration to write, and thank you for helping me live a story worth telling.

I'd also like to say a sincere thank you to my best friends, Joni Bynum and Dayna Abraham, who "handle my crazy" and remind me that my voice matters. Thank you for the late-night chats, the thousand quick questions, and all of the freak out timers.

Beyond that, I'd love to thank Shelley Brewer, my editor, and Cassondra Freeman, my book designer. All of the autistic advocates featured in this book, thank you for sharing your stories, I know that parents reading this will be inspired and comforted.

Finally, a huge thank you for everyone who took the time to read this book and share your journey with me. I'm honored to have shared my thoughts with you, and you are the reason that I write. Keep growing, keep learning, keep embracing autism.

www.ingramcontent.com/pod-product-compliance
Lightning Source LLC
Chambersburg PA
CBHW050918160426
43194CB00011B/2458